THE DAY IT RAINED

A Play by

Phyllis Demaine

Published by:
New Playwrights' Network
35 Sandringham Road
Macclesfield
Cheshire
SK10 1QB

ISBN 0 86319 296 3

Scene. Inside of Noah's house. There is a door opening, slightly left of centre back and another front stage right. Suggestion of a window stage left.

A minimum of plain furniture. A kitchen-type table, set slightly centre right, with three wooden chairs grouped casually round it. Plus a stool, set front stage left, where ADAH is sitting sewing when the curtain rises. To give colour and interest to the set a trestle-type table could be placed back stage right, holding fruit and vegetables which seem applicable to the period, plus, rough baked bread and earthenware type pottery.

Loose costumes in plain colours, corded at the waist and ankle length, with a draped head covering, to mask modern hair styles. REBEKAH, as wife of the Head Counsellor should wear 'royal' purple, with TIMNA in a lighter shade of the same colour. REBEKAH should also wear a chain with a medallion, representing her higher position.

Lighting - normal interior which should begin to dim gradually from DINAH's speech (page 13) 'YOU MEAN GOD WON'T'. As RACHEL makes her closing speech - It was a rare sight etc., centre front, a spot light should be trained on her.

CHARACTERS

RACHEL: Noah's wife. She does not really believe but is loyal to Noah.

DINAH: Shem's wife (first son). Firmly believes.

ADAH: Japath's wife. Frankly sceptical.

LEAH: Ham's wife. Young and uncaring.

SHULAH: Wife of Joseph, the village carpenter.

REBEKAH: Wife of Isaac, Head Councellor in the village.

TIMNA: Rebekah's sister.

SCENE: Inside of Noah's house. Roughly furnished. No attempt at period because nothing is known of furnishings, etc., then.

THE DAY IT RAINED

As the curtain rises ADAH sits sewing. LEAH peeps round the door. She is young and rather flashily dressed with bracelets and jewelry.

LEAH: Pst! Pst! *(ADAH doesn't hear. Whispers)* Adah!

ADAH: What!....Oh, Leah, it's only you. *(Sucks finger)* Look what you've made me do. Why can't you come in properly like other people?

LEAH: *(Sidling in, looking round, hands behind her back)* Where's Mother Rachel?

ADAH: Well she's certainly not hiding. You know you really ought to think before you give people a shock. My finger's bleeding. And what if it had been Mother or Father Noah?

LEAH: *(Laughing)* Then I wouldn't have come in, stupid.

ADAH: Oh, I understand. All right, give it to me. *(Holds out hand)*

LEAH: *(Pretends innocence but one hand still behind her back)* Give you what, Adah?

ADAH: The basin or whatever you've brought to carry home whatever it is you've come to borrow.

LEAH: *(Pulls out basin)* It's only some beans. *(Sulky)* I can't help it if I forget things. *(Sits)* Housekeeping's such a bore. *(Fiddles with bracelets. Brightens)* How do you like my new bracelet)

ADAH: What, another! Has that husband of yours money to throw away?

LEAH: *(Looks sly)* It wasn't Ham.

ADAH: *(Half amused)* Leah! Isn't it time you grew up?

LEAH: *(Twirls about displaying bracelets)* But Adah, it's such fun. And can I help it if the men like to give me things?

ADAH: Just you watch out that one of them doesn't give you something you didn't bargain for. *(Takes basin)* Here, give me that. I'll get the beans for you, then you can go before Mother comes back or Dinah drops in.

LEAH: *(Startled, edges to door)* Dinah! You're not expecting her, are you? Mother's bad enough but that Dinah! She's so stuffy. She'd be bound to notice I had something new. I think she counts my things.

ADAH: *(Laughs)* That's just your guilty conscience. *(Moves to kitchen)* By the way, how would you have got the beans if Mother had been here?

LEAH: Sneaked a few.....I've done it before.

ADAH: And we've been putting down traps for mice. We'll have to change our bait...like a new pair of ear-rings, would you say? *(Both go out, then ADAH comes back after a time. Calling over her shoulder)* And hurry home before you have Ham coming looking for you.

LEAH: *(Voice off)* Oh, don't fuss! You're getting as bad as Mother. *(ADAH sits down to her sewing. Searches for stains)*

ADAH: I hope I haven't marked it. Silly little fool to give me a start like that. *(Smiles)* She's a bit wild, bless her, but she means no harm. nAd she's right, there isn't much fun around these days. *(Sighs)* I wonder where it's all going to end. *(RACHEL bustles in carrying a basket of clothes. Jumping up)* Let me, Mother Rachel. Why don't you give a shout when you're ready. That basket's heavy.

(Takes basket from RACHEL and puts it on the table, then goes back to sewing. RACHEL begins to fold clothes)

RACHEL: For one thing, after doing all that washing I haven't breath for shouting, even if my voice would reach here from the river.

ADAH: You could let me do the washing.

RACHEL: I'd sooner do it myself, then I know it's done properly. Besides, you're neater at sewing than I am. I'll say that for you.

ADAH: *(Aside) Though not much else apparently. (Louder)* Why don't you get Japeth to dig us that well he's been talking about for ever?

RACHEL: Why don't you, since he's your husband now?

ADAH: Oh...you know how it is with these men...there's always tomorrow.

RACHEL: Don't I just! If his father would make me that sledge he's talked of time and again, no one would have to carry it.

DINAH: *(Entering on last words)* Carry what, Mother?

RACHEL: Hallo, Dinah. We were talking about the washing. I was saying if that husband of mine would do something for me for a change...it would be the first time.

DINAH: But Mother, that's not fair. Father Noah is doing something for you. For all of us, come to that.

ADAH: *(Amazed)* You don't mean you believe that tale, Dinah, do you?

DINAH: Of course I do. Shem does.

ADAH: You amaze me! So that's that, is it? What Shem believes must be true.

DINAH: It's not just that. Anyway, you're young yet. You've not been married so long. She'll find out, won't she, Mother? I doesn't do any harm to let them have their own way.

ADAH: I'll not pander to Japeth, whatever you say. And don't make it sound as if that great thing they're building is just some new toy or something.

RACHEL: Now you two!!

ADAH: But Mother! Both your husband's are working on

that...that Ark every minute God sends and you just don't bother. I don't understand.

RACHEL: You've answered it yourself..every minute GOD sends.

ADAH: Oh, Mother!...Well, I don't mean Japeth to waste his time on that crazy scheme.

DINAH: You mustn't speak of it like that, Adah. It's not... not right somehow. I can't explain.

ADAH: Something or someone definitely is not right, that I'll grant you....Building a boat...here...miles from any water.

RACHEL: *(Trying to explain)* Why else would Noah be doing it, if he wasn't told? It's such a lot of work. What kind of man does something like this for no reason? At first I thought like you. I thought it was just his fun when he tried to tell me. Just an excuse for doing all that work...but he's never needed excuses for working before. Now if it was to get out of it....

ADAH: That would be more believable.

DINAH: There's no talking to her.I don't know what's coming over the young people today. When I was a young wife *(ADAH mouths the words with her)* I didn't question what my husband said. When I was young, children were seen and not heard. No wonder they are to be driven from the earth.

ADAH: But we're not. Father has been told to make rooms for us as well. As far as I understand...and I know that isn't far...Japeth and I aren't to be left out. Nor Leah and Ham. I understand it wasn't confined to the young.

DINAH: That's it, everyone but us.

ADAH: That fact alone makes all this harder to believe. I mean, why us? I know the men don't join in all this rough stuff that seems to be the fashion, or get drunk, but we're none of us saints. Take my husband, for instance. The only reason he doesn't run after women is because he's too damn lazy.

RACHEL: *(Laughs)* I think you'd find that's the case with a lot of men.

ADAH: *(Goes to MOTHER)* Seriously. That's the one thing

that makes me doubtful. Father and Shem, they're not the world's hardest workers, yet they have been slaving away for months. It's unnatural.

DINAH: Yet you won't believe the truth?

ADAH: I can't.

LEAH: *(Coming in)* Hallo. What's this? Family conclave? Mother, is Father about?

RACHEL: Hallo, dear. No. Did you expect to find him here? He'll be down in the field.

LEAH: I couldn't see him.

ADAH: *(Leaning close)* What did you run out of this time?

LEAH: Adah, don't be mean. I really do want father. Ham can't manage those animals.

RACHEL: What! Ham? He's never had any difficulty before. Always had such a way with sheep.

LEAH: Yes, and I'm beginning to wish he hadn't, then Father wouldn't have given him this job.

RACHEL: What job's this? The animals have always been his responsibility.

LEAH: But there's a lot of difference between a few silly sheep and some wild pigs.

ADAH: Wild pigs! Whatever does he want them for?

DINAH: For the Ark, of course.

ADAH: The Ark!

DINAH: Do stop repeating everything. There has got to be two of every kind of animal.

ADAH: This thing gets crazier by the minute.

DINAH: *(To LEAH)* But I don't see his problem. Those dogs of Ham's are pretty fierce. I can't see them running away from the odd pig.

LEAH: That's just it. There wouldn't be any problem if it was the ODD pig. It's this business of pairs.

DINAH: Yes, I suppose that would complicate matters.

ADAH: Look. Would someone tell me what all this is about? I can see two pigs are harder to handle than one but once he's got them in the pen.....?

LEAH: There's more to it than that. It's...You tell her, Dinah.

DINAH: There has to be two of each kind...male and female.. so they'll...you know...breed.

ADAH: And Ham's having trouble finding out which is which. *(Laughs)*

RACHEL: Now Adah!

ADAH: But a grown man!

RACHEL: I said that was enough. You should stay away from that well in the village. There's too much loose talk goes on down there.

ADAH: Not any more. I don't go. The only thing they all talk about is us. I don't like being laughed at.

RACHEL: Laughed at?

LEAH: It's true, Mother. Since Father started building the Ark we've become the laughing stock of the village. It wasn't so bad at first. I used to say it was a boat...for him and the others to go fishing.

ADAH: I bet they believed you. Why this river wouldn't float a good sized duck, let alone a boat. Never mind one as big as that thing, even before they added the top stories. *(To DINAH)* That's a thought, Dinah; you seem to know a lot about this project. How is father proposing to get it into some water?

DINAH: He won't need to...It's going to rain.

RACHEL: Is that right? But won't it need a terrible lot of water to bring the river here? It's ten minutes good walkaway, as I know only too well.

DINAH: That's what he was told. It is going to rain for forty days. *(RACHEL makes for the door)* Mother! Where are you going?

RACHEL: I'd better go and get the washing I left by the river.

LEAH: *(Laughs)* She doesn't mean right away.

RACHEL: All the same, I'd better go. You never know...Forty days, you said. That ought to be enough even for Noah. *(Exit RACHEL)*

DINAH: Oh, dear. I suppose I should go and help. *(Exit DINAH)*

LEAH: *(Goes to window)* Don't you really believe it all, Adah?

ADAH: Do you?

LEAH: I don't know what to believe any longer. They all seem so sure. Father Noah and Shem and now Dinah.

Even Mother's gone to fetch the washing. *(Both laugh)* And why else should they do all that? If there isn't a flood it will all be wasted. They're going to be awful mad.

ADAH: Have you ever known that river to rise above an inch, even in a bad winter?

LEAH: No...but...

ADAH: Well then! And as for it raining forty days and forty nights...it just isn't possible, though it would certainly need every drop to float that great hulking structure. Have you taken a look at it lately?

LEAH: I keep well away. I don't want Noah finding me jobs. He roped me in when they were putting on the pitch. Ugh! Horrible, it was.

ADAH: You should take a look. It's a days walk round it, believe me. I do it quite regularly...good for the figure, you understand. *(Someone knocks)* Who ever can that be? We don't get many callers nowadays. Mother doesn't say much but it's obvious she's missing her old friends. I don't know when Shulah and Rebekah were here last. *(She goes to the door)* Oh...er...Rebekah. We were just saying it's a long time since some of Mother's friends dropped by. And now you've just missed her. But do come in. *(ADAH returns, followed by REBEKAH and TIMNA)*

LEAH: *(Gets up)* Hallo, Rebekah. Mother will be pleased to see you.

REBEKAH: I doubt that. *(Sits)* To tell the truth I'm not sorry to have missed her. I'd rather hoped to catch you girls alone.

ADAH: Indeed! Now I wonder why.

REBEKAH: Don't use that tone with me, Miss! I'm, entitled to respect. They didn't make my husband Head Counsellor for nothing.

ADAH: Certainly not for nothing..ten sheep was the figure, I heard.

TIMNA: My sister deserves some respect...her position, you know.

ADAH: *(Looks at REBEKAH sprawled)* Yes, I can see what you

mean. *(To REBEKAH)* What do you want to talk to us about?

REBEKAH: I don't quite know how to put it. You know I don't like interfering. But I do have the goodness of the village at heart. And what I mean is...it has got to stop.

TIMNA: Yes, my sister's right. Someone should put a stop to it.

LEAH: I don't think we understand. What has got to stop?

REBEKAH: All this building your Father's doing.

ADAH: *(Aside)* And she says she doesn't like interfering. *(Aloud)* I don't see what we can do about it.

TIMNA: Someone must, before it's too late. The Counsellors..... *(REBEKAH silences her with a look)*

SHULAH: *(Coming in)* Your Mother said to come right in...... sorry, I didn't know you had visitors. But your Mother did say....

LEAH: Is your Mother with you?

SHULAH: No...I saw her down at that building of your Father's.....

ADAH: The Ark.

SHULAH: Ark? *(Sniffs)* Is that what he calls it. Great waste of good wood if you ask me.

ADAH: We didn't.

SHULAH: Anyway, your Mother said to come in as she wouldn't be long.

REBEKAH: If your mother's going to be back soon we'd better have our little talk, hadn't we? Get things sorted out.

LEAH: What do you want us to talk about? Father won't stop building, you know.

REBEKAH: Is the fellow quite mad? Tell me. Is he? It's the maddest thing I've ever heard of.

TIMNA: Exceedingly foolish, to say the least. But that family, Rebekah dear. There was always something...

REBEKAH: *(Sharply)* Be quiet, Timna..er..better leave this to me.

SHULAH: That is just what I said. The man must be mad, I told Joseph. Using all that good timber. *(Turns to the girls)* Do you know there isn't a cubit of wood to be got, not anywhere. And what's my Joseph to do if he can't get timber? Tell me that. A carpenter's not much use if he's not got a scrap of wood to work at. Trade's fallen off something shocking.

ADAH: I'm sorry. But what do you imagine we can do about it?

TIMNA: You can stop your father. Take away his hammer or his saw, or something. He couldn't go on then. *(Triumphantly)*

LEAH: But he has to build the Ark. He has to. God told him.

REBEKAH: I'm glad you were the one to say that; that you brought it into the open. There's a lot of talk in the village. My husband doesn't like it. He doesn't like it at all. Gives the place a bad name. Word gets around, you know. It doesn't look well for Isaac, having a mad man in the village.

LEAH: But Noah's not mad.

REBEKAH: What else would you call it. Of course he's mad.

TIMNA: Yes, he must be...mad as a coot. Like his uncle. He used to take off all his clothes and run through the village.

SHULAH: That's what I've said all along. Mad as can be.

ADAH: He may be a little...well...misguided...but...

REBEKAH: My dear Adah, are you going to stand there and tell me you believe all this nonsense about the rain coming and everything.

ADAH: What I believe doesn't come into it. Father believes, and I seem to remember hearing you say that children should honour their parents.

LEAH: And my husband believes it. He's sorting out the animals.

SHULAH: Animals? What animals?

REBEKAH: Yes. Don't change the subject, child. What have animals to do with all this?

LEAH: God told Noah to build the Ark and make rooms for all the family and then he must make places for the animals.

REBEKAH: You keep on talking about animals. What animals? Explain yourself, child.

ADAH: It's all of them. There was something about things that crawl and things that walk...oh...every kind.

TIMNA: I'm certainly glad I'm not coming. I shouldn't want to live with a lot of dirty animals. So unhygenic.

ADAH: You aren't invited.

REBEKAH: Now I know that Noah's mad. That proves it beyond a shadow of a doubt. Noah's mad!

RACHEL: *(Coming in, hears this. DINAH follows and goes to rear of room. She starts absent-mindedly to fold clothes)* Mad! Who dares to say my husband is mad?

REBEKAH: Well isn't he?

RACHEL: Don't be ridiculous....and unkind too. You've known Noah for years. How can you say these things? I'm sorry, Rebekah, I know your husband is Head Counsellor but it doesn't give you the right to say such things, especially not under his own roof.

REBEKAH: I'm sure I respect his ROOF. But look at it this way, Rachel. Surely if God had put this idea into anyone's head he would have chosen my husband. After all, he is Head Counsellor and this is supposed to be for the good of the whole village.

DINAH: It's to save the world.

TIMNA: The very idea! Noah to save the world. Why I've known him all my life.

REBEKAH: That's what I mean. For such a project God would have chosen somebody of importance. Not some little nobody. Isaac's Head Counsellor.

ADAH: We had gathered that. I can't think how.

REBEKAH: So if anybody had to do it, it would be Isaac.

RACHEL: How do I know why Noah was chosen.

TIMNA: But Isaac should have been consulted. At the very least he should have been asked.

ADAH: What does Isaac know about building? He's never done a day's hard work in his life.

TIMNA: And quite right too. Some people aren't born to it. Some people are meant for higher things.

SHULAH: If we're talking of suitability, why not Joseph? He is the best carpenter around here. Never mind your Isaac being Head Counsellor. Stands to reason, if God wanted that great wooden boat building... and mind I only said if...he'd have chosen a proper carpenter. All that wood-work. Stands to reason.

REBEKAH: There seems little reason about any of this as far as I can see. These girls tell me Noah's going to fill it with a lot of animals.

TIMNA: Never could abide pigs and things myself.

LEAH: But of course there must be animals. What would we do for food afterwards if there were no animals when the water goes down?

REBEKAH: Oh, Leah, my dear girl. Won't you listen to your elders and betters? You're new to this family...perhaps you can still see sense. Of course there isn't going to be a flood. Of course God didn't speak to your father. It is all some strange idea he has got into his head, poor man. I suppose he should be pitied.

RACHEL: But it's not...You don't know, Rebekah..You didn't.. Why can't I make you see?

ADAH: *(Cutting her short)* Father is putting rather a lot of work into this, if it's just a whim. He works at it every minute there is daylight. Doesn't come home for his food at mid-day. He says he can't spare the time.

SHULAH: That only bears out what I was saying to Joseph. There's more in this mad idea of Noah's, I said, than meets the eye. Maybe there is some other reason why he just can't spend too much time here. Maybe he wants to be...well...out of the way...

RACHEL: *(Turns on her)* Shulah Joseph! Just what are you implying?

SHULAH: I'm sorry, dear. But some things have to be said. You always did have a sharp tongue in your head, Rachel. Didn't your own father say the same thing on your wedding day? Don't nag, Rachel, he said. You're a good lass but you are too much like your mother. And he was right. Many's the time I've heard you going on and on at Noah.

RACHEL: You had better go, Shulah, before I do something I'll be sorry for.

TIMNA: But it is true, Rachel. Men don't like a wife who

nags. Our mother....rest her soul...always used to say that, didn't she, Rebekah?

REBEKAH: *(Silences her)* Now look here, both of you. This is no time to quarrel. *(She goes to RACHEL)* Rachel's going to need all of us, especially now.

RACHEL: I don't see....

DINAH: *(Coming forward to get hold of REBEKAH's arm)* What have you done? What *have* you done? *(REBEKAh jerks away)* You and your precious Counsellor.

REBEKAH: *(Bridles and moves away)* Only our duty. We are only acting for the best.

ADAH: Did you say duty? That word has an ugly sound.

REBEKAH: Isn't it the Counsellor's duty to look after the interests of the village?

ADAH: It depends.

REBEKAH: How do you define that duty if a mad dog gets loose?

RACHEL: You don't mean...No, you can't? But Noah's not mad. I tell you he's not. *(She turns to DINAH)* Tell them, Dinah. You were there just now. Tell them.

DINAH: No, Mother, not now. It isn't the time.

REBEKAH: The Counsellor's have decided that Noah isn't...... responsible.

ADAH: So now it's the whole Counsel? I don't doubt the *head* Counsellor had something to do with it...and his wife. I think you're jealous, Rebekah.

REBEKAH: Whatever do I have to be jealous of? *(Looks round the room)* I keep telling you, Isaac, they were all, only doing their duty.

SHULAH: Anyway, they took a vote, Joseph said.

ADAH: So you're in this too. I might have known.

DINAH: *(Disbelieving)* You, Shulah? I can understand Rebekah, but you? You were always mother's friend. Father Noah and Joseph, they were like brothers!

LEAH: Until Father cornered the market in wood. That's the way of it, isn't it, Shulah? She thinks God should have chosen a carpenter, Dinah.

DINAH: *(A cry for help)* Oh, God!

ADAH: I'm beginning to see why it has to happen. *(More to self)*

REBEKAH: *(In desperation and exasperation)* Nothing is going to happen. Will you get that into your heads? Nothing, I tell you. At least not in the way you mean...The counsellors will be coming soon...for Noah...not for you. Isaac let me come first to warn you, to make it easier.

RACHEL: You think there is an easy way to take a woman's husband away? That telling me first makes it all right? *(RACHEL sits at the table)* My poor Noah. My poor Noah.

LEAH: *(Going to RACHEL)* Don't cry, Mother. We won't let them hurt him.

DINAH: *(Turns from window)* You mean God won't.

TIMNA: Don't blaspheme, dear. It isn't nice.

DINAH: I think you had better go. You too, Shulah. You've done enough damage. *(Can't resist dig)* And the wagons won't wait all day.

LEAH: What wagons?

ADAH: Yes. What other schemes have they been hatching?

TIMNA: *(Prepares to retreat)* Dear, dear. I knew we should never have come.

DINAH: Only their own escape. *(Laughs ironically)* It's funny, really. They don't believe it but they are all packed up and ready to go, to leave the village.

TIMNA: Did you expect us to drown?

ADAH: And what was to happen to us? At least Noah told you of God's plan and asked you along.

REBEKAH: You can come with us. *(Placatingly)* My husband pleaded that you might join us. There are those who wanted it differently *(sly look at SHULAH)* but Isaac stuck out....Of course....Noah!

DINAH: He was to be shut away.

SHULAH: You can't expect us to take a lunatic with us.

TIMNA: No indeed! You can't expect that.....all us women.

ADAH: *(Scornfully)* I think your virtue is safe, Timna.

LEAH: But where are you going?

REBEKAH: Up into the hills. We'll be safe there until the rain stops.

LEAH: But you don't believe! You say Father's mad! You can't have it both ways.

DINAH: Of course they don't believe Father, but they can't

be sure. You haven't been outside, have you? But surely you've noticed it is going dark? And the river...that's already twice its width. I suppose it has been raining up in the mountains for some time.

SHULAH: *(Moves to LEAH)* So you see you must come. You're nearer to the river than any of us. I don't think you can bank on that Ark floating...Of course if Joseph had been asked....There won't be time to pack much but I'm sure we could find room for some food and bits of things.

RACHEL: But it's no use. I tell you, if you had seen... *(RACHEL tries to pull REBEKAH to the window)* Rebekah....come. Perhaps you can see from here. *(REBEKAH pulls back, a little alarmed)*

DINAH: *(Pulls her mother away and REBEKAH steps further back)* No, Mother. *(Quietly)* Let them go. *(The family close up as they watch the others go with backward glances of wonderment)*

LEAH: *(Sits down wearily)* I'm glad they've gone.

ADAH: Dinah, what did happen out there? What did you and Mother see?

DINAH: The Ark is finished.

ADAH: *(Impatiently)* Yes, yes, I guessed that. Father said it would be ready today.

DINAH: And it is raining. And the river is rising.

LEAH: But I thought that was what you expected. You always believed.

DINAH: Perhaps...I'm not sure any longer. Oh, I know I said....But when you see for yourself.....

ADAH: What? For God's sake tell us what you saw.

RACHEL: Aye...for God's sake....or man's...I don't know.

LEAH: *(Jumps up hysterically)* Tell us. Please. Do tell us. Father and Ham...they're all right?

RACHEL: *(Puts her arm around LEAH)* Yes, my child, hush. They're safe. There's no need to fret. *(RACHEL looks out front)* It was strange though. Like Dinah says, I believed and yet I didn't. It was so fantastic. But so fantastic it had to be true. But when we saw the animals...*(She turns back to LEAH, laughing slightly at her)*...and your Ham had been having all that trouble with them, poor boy...Even Noah had his unbelief. He didn't altogether trust God.

ADAH: Not Father. He was the only one.

RACHEL: No, not completely. Not far enough. Didn't he put Ham to catching the animals? He was meant to leave that to God...I stood by Noah as the came. Two by two as God had said. Things that walked and things that slithered. Things that crawled and those that flew. Every mortal living thing. Quiet as lambs they came. Up the gangplank and down into the holds...as if they knew.

ADAH: *(Subdued)* Perhaps they did.

LEAH: Mother! Mother Rachel! I'm frightened! *(She goes to RACHEL)*

RACHEL: *(Comforts LEAH a moment, then turns briskly)* Come along then. We've a lot to do. I don't suppose the good Lord meant us to go into the Ark empty handed. He made all the other provisions, now it's up to us. *(RACHEL gathers up clothes, stops off centre)* It was a rare sight though. A wonderful sight. You won't see the like, not in a million years. *(Exit RACHEL. The others take up bundles and follow slowly)*

CURTAIN